Propitiation

1st John 4:7-12

[7] Beloved, let us love one another,
for love is from God, and whoever
loves has been born of God and
knows God. [8] Anyone who does not
love does not know God,
because God is love. [9] In this the
love of God was made manifest
among us, that God sent his only Son
into the world, so that we might live
through him. [10] In this is love, not
that we have loved God but that he
loved us and sent his Son to be the
propitiation for our sins. [11] Beloved,
if God so loved us, we also ought to
love one another. [12] No one has ever
seen God; if we love one another,
God abides in us and his love is
perfected in us.

There is a lot you could talk about in these verses but let us focus on the big word here propitiation! This word means the action of pleasing a god, spirit, or person.

This is something none of us can do. Not one of us can please God for our sins. So let me put it this way: I know some people who have served time in prison and if you have, you'll know what I am talking about. Going before the judge and standing there with your attorney as the verdict comes in guilty as charged. Then the sentencing is about to come, and you know that because of the crime you may be looking at a long time behind bars, but just as the judge says 25 years, a man stands up from the courtroom audience and says, "I'd like to serve that time in their place."

Could you imagine the feeling? Can you feel the emotions you'd feel of someone offering to serve your time? What would you say as the judge said okay and they unshackled you and showed you the door? As the man walked to take your place, would you be grateful? Would you live a better life?

This is propitiation, and it has been done for all who believe!

Would you pray with me today? Lord, thank you that Christ stood in my place. Thank you that you are a gracious God and help me to live a life for you today. Lord, help me to realize the freedom you gave me today! Amen.

Called Holy

1st Peter 1:15-16

15 But just as He who called you is holy, so be holy in all you do; 16 for it is written: "Be holy, because I am holy."

My favorite sport in the world is wrestling and I am a wrestler. Although I do not practice wrestling much nowadays, once you have wrestled you are always a wrestler. Just when do you become a wrestler, or how do you *become* a wrestler. You can buy shoes and wear the uniform and look like a wrestler but you are not a wrestler. It is the moments after you have worked your butt off in the practice room and walked out sweaty, bruised, and dead tired. It is also the moment you step on the mat to face an opponent just you versus him and now you put into practice all you have learned. Then you are a wrestler!

I have heard the question asked, "When are you holy."

Well, I am here to tell you the minute you repent and begin to walk for Christ, you are holy. At that very moment, God no longer looks at you as unholy; He views you through the blood-stained eyes of Christ washed and cleaned by the blood. You are holy today! The minute you stumble and confess your sin and repent you are made holy. Christ clothes you in His righteousness so you can be holy. You are a son, a daughter, a child of God and He has made you holy!

Would you pray with me today? Lord, help me to view myself as you view me. Help me to see myself clothed in the righteousness that you have covered me in. Lord, help me to live that holy life that you have for me. Amen.

The Secret

1st Samuel 17:34-36

34 But David said to Saul, "Your servant used to keep sheep for his father. And when there came a lion, or a bear, and took a lamb from the flock, 35 I went after him and struck him and delivered it out of his mouth. And if he arose against me, I caught him by his beard and struck him and killed him. 36 Your servant has struck down both lions and bears, and this uncircumcised Philistine shall be like one of them, for he has defied the armies of the living God."

It takes years of training to be good at something. If you are an athlete, you train for years in your sport before reaching the pinnacle. If you are a student, you spend hours studying in secret to ace the test. If you are an employee, you spend your weeks learning and mastering the skills needed to climb the corporate ladder. Ultimately, you make it to the top of whatever your skill is by the work done when nobody sees you.

David spent much of his time as a boy alone with the sheep. I imagine much of the time was spent talking with God and when the battles came, he knew who to rely on. It was those secret battles over the years that gave David the courage and strength to stand against the giant. It was all that time David spent walking with the Lord in secret that gave him confidence to stand when no one else would.

What are you doing in secret? Are you spending time with the Lord or are you wasting it away? How many of those secret battles have you won with the strength of the Lord? Remember those victories and walk in them into many new victories beginning today!

Would you pray with me? Lord, you have given me victory over so much in secret and now I ask you to remind me of those victories as I face new battles. Please give me the strength to overcome new challenges in my path. Help me to stand against my giants today. Thank you, Lord!

Stand Your Ground

1st Samuel 17:31-32

31 When the words which David spoke were heard, they told *them* to Saul, and he sent for him. 32 David said to Saul, "Let no man's heart fail on account of him; your servant will go and fight with this Philistine."

Almost three weeks after the events of 9-1,1 there was a transformer explosion in the Hartford Civic Center. I just happened to be walking through the skywalk to the parking garage when this took place. People were on high alert with the terror attacks happening just a few weeks before, and rightfully so.

As I walked there was a man in a suit walking next to me talking on his cell phone. As he was just passing me there was a loud bang and the building shook. The lights went out and people began screaming. In a single motion the man dropped his cell phone in his pocket and took off in a dead sprint. I don't know why but I paused for a moment and looked around before running. I guess it was to make sure which way was the safest to go. So, I started to run, but as soon as I could see the door of the parking garage I heard some teenagers yelling. Everything in my mind was telling me to run for my car and get out of there, but in my heart I knew I had to make sure they were alright. So, I turned and ran to the escalators which were now stuck, and as I got to the top of them, a security guard saw me and yelled "I got them" and "Get out of here!" So, I bolted for my car and drove as fast as I could home.

What is our response to evil? What is our response to the battle of our carnal desires? What is our response to the attacks from the enemy on our soul?

In a dangerous situation people do one of three things. They either run for their lives, or become paralyzed by fear, or they fight danger.

You know the story these verses come from. The Israelites were paralyzed by fear of the giant Philistine. They allowed him to come out and mock them day after day. They were God's chosen people, but they allowed an agent of Satan to take away their strength.

Do we do the same today? Do we give ground to the world because of fear? I certainly have a lot of times. Do we allow our desires to sap our strength away from the battle? Do we allow the enemy to slowly break our faith down until we flee from the One who loves us?

This is our struggle as believers in Christ and we must stand in fight! You must make the choice: I will not lay paralyzed and be the victim of evil! You must decide in your heart: I will not run from things that do not have power over me, but I will stand my ground and fight for whatever little I have.

Stand and Fight

2nd Timothy 1:7 tells us "For God has not given us a spirit of fear, but of power and of love and of a sound mind."

We know if it is in God's word that it is a promise for us! It is truth. You, me, and the rest of the body around the world are warriors and need not fear anything because Christ lives in us! Stand and fight with me today! Stand and fight for that which God gave you!

Let's pray! Oh Lord God, you are mighty to save and have conquered all things. You are the King of Kings and Lord of Host! I pray that you strengthen me for battle today. I pray that you give my victory over my doubts and fears. I pray for victory over temptations and sins in my life. I thank you Lord and praise your holy name. Amen

Battles

2nd Chronicles 20:14-17

***14* Then the Spirit of the LORD came on Jahaziel son of Zechariah, the son of Benaiah, the son of Jeiel, the son of Mattaniah, a Levite and descendant of Asaph, as he stood in the assembly.**

***15* He said: "Listen, King Jehoshaphat and all who live in Judah and Jerusalem! This is what the LORD says to you: 'Do not be afraid or discouraged because of this vast army. For the battle is not**
***yours, but God's. 16 Tomorrow march down against them. They will be climbing up by the Pass of Ziz, and you will find them at the end of the**
gorge in the Desert of Jeruel. 17 You will not have to fight this battle. Take up your positions; stand firm and see the deliverance the LORD will give you, Judah and Jerusalem. Do not be afraid; do not be discouraged.

***Go out to face them tomorrow, and the* L*ORD* *will be with you*.'"**

I have been in a few scraps in my day, and I can remember the nerves before the battle; wondering if I was getting into something I shouldn't? Can I take this guy down? What do I do if I get my butt kicked? Maybe you have been there in a battle that you knew you just couldn't win. What do you do with that?

If you're smart, you high tail it out of there and live to fight another day, but Jehoshaphat didn't have that option. So, Jehoshaphat did the only thing he could do and turned to the Lord. Then the Lord answered through Jahaziel and reminded all of them that the battle was not Jehoshaphat's or anyone else's; it was the Lord's.

What kind of battle are you going through today? What is leaving you feeling discouraged and down? Does it feel like enemies are closing in all around you?

Well, do what Jehoshaphat did in the previous verses: fast and pray. Be open with those closest to you about the battle you are in and be transparent with them. Maybe, and most likely, the Lord has a Jahaziel to speak a word of encouragement and direction into your life so you might have victory over what seems impossible.

Will you pray with me today? Lord, please show me the right people to speak with about my battles. Lord, would you please send an encourager into my life. Help me to have the courage to speak about my battles to those closest around me. Protect me from judgements and discouragement. Amen!

Heirs of the Kingdom

2nd Corinthians 5:17

17 Therefore if anyone is in Christ, *he is* a new creature; the old things passed away; behold, new things have come.

James 2:5

5 Listen, my beloved brethren: did not God choose the poor of this world *to be* rich in faith and heirs of the kingdom which He promised to those who love Him?

1st John 4:4

4 You are from God, little children, and have overcome them; because greater is He who is in you than he who is in the world.

I have recently become interested in tracing my family's genealogy. I have found that I can trace back over 1,000 years. The reason I am doing this is because I find a need to know more about just who my family is and who I am. I have this urge to know about my heritage and just what my bloodline is. I would say I just wanted to know who I am.

Have you ever felt like this? I wonder who I am and where I came from. What is my history?

I think sometimes we may feel like this when it comes to our walk with Christ. I would be confident in saying some of us wonder just what is our heritage in Christ?

Well, if you are a believer in Christ today, then you have no need to doubt. Just like the verse from Corinthians says you are a new creature in Christ. In Christ your past no longer matters. Your sins and your heritage of sin is broken.

You no longer need to search the archives of history to see if you belong to royalty or that you may be an heir to a kingdom of the world, because you who love Christ are heirs to the greatest kingdom in the universe. You are prince and princesses to the kingdom of God!

I know some of you are thinking I don't feel that way and this can't be me but read the verse from 1st John and believe it. This verse is for you today! You who believe in Christ are from God and He who lives in you is greater than the world, greater than the doubt, greater than the sin that is besetting you. He has overcome and today is the day for you to let Him overcome in your life!

Let us pray today. Lord Jesus, help me to know and believe you have overcome all things in my life today at this very moment! Help me to walk in the confidence of royalty as an heir to the kingdom. Lord, please help to see I am a new creature and more than what I think I am! Amen.

Consequences

2nd Samuel 12:19-23

***19 But when David saw that his
servants were whispering together,
David understood that the child was
dead. And David said to his servants,
"Is the child dead?" They said, "He is
dead." 20 Then David arose from the
earth and washed and anointed
himself and changed his clothes. And
he went into the house of the
LORD and worshipped. He then went
to his own house. And when he
asked, they set food before him, and
he ate. 21 Then his servants said to
him, "What is this thing that you
have done? You fasted and wept for
the child while he was alive; but
when the child died, you arose and
ate food." 22 He said, "While the child
was still alive, I fasted and wept, for
I said, 'Who knows whether
the LORD will be gracious to me, that
the child may live?' 23 But now he is
dead. Why should I fast? Can I bring***

him back again? I shall go to him, but he will not return to me."

There was a boy and when he was growing up, he would get in trouble occasionally. His father had a rock pile outside the house that was going to be used to build a rock wall and whenever this boy would get in trouble the father would say "you know I think I might start that rock wall this week". The father would then send the boy to move the rock pile from one end of the yard to the other. That boy would carry each stone one by one and create a new pile is a consequence for his misbehavior.

Don't you just hate consequences?

There are consequences for everything in life. Consequences for sin that never go away even when we come to the Lord, He doesn't just erase all the consequences for our bad behavior, but what the Lord does is help us through them.

You have a choice in life. When you walk with the Lord and that is to hide your troubles for fear of the consequences or confess them and accept your consequence. The great thing about the Lord is He does not look to punish us for our sins, but rather He looks to show us mercy and grace.

It is okay to pray for the consequences to pass just as David did but when the Lord answers accept them and begin to move forward. God wants to do a great work in your life, and it begins with confession and accepting the Lord's will for it!

Let's pray! Lord, help me not to be afraid to accept the consequences for my actions. Help me to confess anything that you lay on my heart, so that I may move forward with you. Please put godly people into my life that will show me mercy in my circumstances and help build me up as I confess my sins. Amen.

Ordinary!

Amos 7:14-15

14 Then Amos answered and said to Amaziah, "I was no prophet, nor a prophet's son, but I was a herdsman and a dresser of sycamore figs. 15 But the LORD took me from following the flock, and the LORD said to me, 'Go, prophesy to my people Israel.'

Many of us get up every day and head out to work between the hours of 6 and 9 AM. We drive in rush hour traffic and go with the flow. We get to the office and sit in our cubicles or get to the job site and set about doing our task. We put in our 8 to 10 hours and get back in our cars and back in that rush hour traffic going with the flow until we get home.

We are information technology guys, mechanics, plumbers, engineers, businessmen, etc.... We follow the flock to bring home the proverbial bacon to take care of our families. There is nothing wrong with this in itself.

Oh, but you know there is more to it than this. We are a people set apart. We are different from the flock. We are different from the flow. We are to be people of the Word; Men of faith, accountable to a different standard, and our attitudes should stand out.

When we go to work, we go on time; we don't take advantage of the system when others do; we do things with a smile; and give thanks to the Lord for our little space. When we do these things, God pulls us out of the flock. People began to notice you are different. They begin to listen to you speak. Your words hold weight because your actions in the flock have allowed God to separate you from it.

Then when asked why you are different or what gives you the right to speak truth, you can answer as Amos answered, I was just an engineer or electrician or insert your job here, but the Lord called me and set me apart. Then you can speak what the Lord has spoken to you in those quiet moments and in those hours of prayer in rush hour traffic. While we work, we are no one special to the world, but how we obey makes us special in the sight of the One that matters.

Would you pray with me today? Lord, help me to do my job well. Help me to be an example and not a complainer. Give me a good attitude when it would be so easy to be negative. I thank you for providing for me and I pray you will give me an opportunity today to be more than just an engineer, electrician, mechanic, etc.... but that I may be a witness today. Please use me to bring that co-worker of mine to faith whether by word or deed. Amen!

Short Time

Ecclesiastes 3:1-8

**1There is an appointed time for
everything. And there is a time for
every event under heaven—**

**2 A time to give birth and a time to
die;
A time to plant and a time to uproot
what is planted.
3 A time to kill and a time to heal;
A time to tear down and a time to
build up.
4 A time to weep and a time to laugh;
A time to mourn and a time to dance.
5 A time to throw stones and a time
to gather stones;
A time to embrace and a time to
shun embracing.
6 A time to search and a time to give
up as lost;
A time to keep and a time to throw
away.
7 A time to tear apart and a time to**

sew together;
A time to be silent and a time to speak.
8 A time to love and a time to hate;
A time for war and a time for peace.

I am in the middle of my life now, and time has just seemed to slip away. I was thinking of my teenage years, the friends I had and how close we were. Now I only ever really speak to one of them and it's only ever so often. Time has truly separated us. I have family, not immediate, cousins and uncles that I rarely have contact with. Time has truly separated us.

I read these words of Solomon, and I must agree there is a time for everything, but why is time such a cruel thing? We all get the same amount of time in a day but are limited to a very short amount of time in terms of eternity. Years ago, you could have never convinced me that time would separate me and my friends or family, but it has.

This is where I get scared to think about our time on earth and our time in eternity. Once this life is over and we begin our new life in eternity, will I be separated from those I love? Will I be separated from my family and friends just as on earth?

Well, that depends on their choices and whether they choose to live for Christ, and I choose to live for Christ. I may not be able to make them believe in Christ with all my intelligence and arguments or by trying to get them to fear eternal damnation in hell, but I can choose to live for Christ in my own life. I can choose to let Christ so fill me that His love becomes infectious and begins to alter my view of time and what really matters.

Would you pray with me today? Oh Lord, please help me not to waste my short time in this life? Help me to live for you and know you more, so that I might help those closest to me and those around me to make the right choice for eternity. Thank you, Jesus! Amen.

Imitation Wanted

Ephesians 5:1-2

Therefore, be imitators of God, as beloved children. [2] And walk in love, as Christ loved us and gave himself up for us, a fragrant offering and sacrifice to God.

Did you ever watch a movie or an athlete and really want to be like the actor or athlete? You know how you would walk around and dress like the movie character and say the things the actor said. You would imitate their mannerisms and speech patterns. You did these things because you thought they were cool! If you could just make that play like that football player, or sing like that singer, wouldn't you be cool too.

What if instead of imitating athletes and movie stars we imitated Christ? How would the world around us look? What would people think about us?

The great news is you can imitate Christ and He will send the Holy Spirit to make it possible for you to be even more like Him. You, as believers in Christ have been given a great ability as an imitator. You have a great model before you of how to act toward one another and toward those whc do not believe. You have been given the ability to walk in love and to give up yourself and selfish ways, all to be an imitation. By becoming an imitation of Christ, you become much more like the real thing. While you may never be a famous actor or athlete, you can be more and more Christ like every day.

Will you pray with me today? Dear Lord Jesus, will you please help me to be more like you? Give me more of your Spirit so that I may be more of an imitation than ever. Help me to walk in love toward my neighbors, family, brothers, and sisters in Christ. Help me to be the real deal, Lord! Amen.

Not My Problem

Esther 4:12-14

[12] When Esther's words were reported to Mordecai, [13] he sent back this answer: "Do not think that because you are in the king's house you alone of all the Jews will escape. [14] For if you remain silent at this time, relief and deliverance for the Jews will arise from another place, but you and your father's family will perish. And who knows but that you have come to your royal position for such a time as this?"

I love comic book movies and some of you may have seen the original Spiderman movie so you will know what I am talking about and for others let me explain. Peter Parker (Spiderman) gained his superhuman strength and decided to use it to make money. He saw an ad for a wrestling match and if he won, he got 3,000 dollars. Well of course he wins the match because he has spider strength but when he goes to collect the money the promoter only gives him 100 dollars. The scene plays out as Peter Parker is walking away and a gunman robs the promoter and runs by Peter Parker as the promoter yells stop him. The following dialogue ensues after the Robber gets away:

Wrestling Promoter: [*after Peter lets an armed man escape with a bag full of cash*] You could have taken that guy apart! Now he's going to get away with *my* money!

Peter Parker: I missed the part where that's my problem.

Shortly after this Peter Parker hears sirens and runs to see what has happened and finds his uncle lying on the sidewalk with a gunshot wound. His uncle ultimately dies.

Remember Peter Parker said to the promoter "I missed the part where that's my problem." when he could have easily stopped the thief.

Esther was put into a position where she could affect the world around her, but it might possibly cost her life. In verse 14 it makes it clear that if she did nothing and just said I missed the part where that's my problem God would find someone else, but her family would not receive the reward.

The world is going to hell all around us. Just turn on the news and you must wonder what is going on. What will make it stop?

We all have been given greater power than any make-believe power in comic book movies. All who have believed on Jesus have the power of the Holy Spirit living within them and all of us have been placed in positions for such a time as this.

You and the Holy Spirit pouring through your veins, pumping the very presence of God through your heart can affect the world around us.

Will you watch the world go to hell and just say "I missed the part where that's my problem." Or will you rise up seek the will of God for your life and find out why you are in this royal position?

Will you pray with me?

Father, you have blessed me with much. Show me how to use my materials, riches, and talents in a time such as this. Show me how I can affect real change on this day. Help me to see the opportunities around me today? Help me to speak when I need to speak, to give when I need to give, and to love the way you love. Amen

Grumblings

Exodus 15:22-26

22 Then Moses made Israel set out
from the Red Sea, and they went
into the wilderness of Shur. They
went three days in the wilderness
and found no water.23 When they
came to Marah, they could not drink
the water of Marah because it was
bitter; therefore, it was named
Marah. 24 And the people grumbled
against Moses, saying, "What shall
we drink?" 25 And he cried to
the LORD, and the LORD showed him a
log, and he threw it into the water,
and the water became sweet.

There the LORD made for them a statute and a rule, and there
he tested them,26 saying, "If you will
diligently listen to the voice of the LORD your God, and do that which is right in his eyes, and give ear to his commandments and keep all his statutes, I will put none of

the diseases on you that I put on the Egyptians, for I am the LORD, your healer."

I remember there was a particular politician when I was a younger man that I thought was going to be a great leader. I believed he was going to lead this country in the right direction. As his time in the office went on, I became disappointed. I was not so much disappointed in him as a man, but he was not the leader I hoped he would be. The country did not get better under his leadership, and I even began to grumble.

In the passage above we see the Israelites following a man they put their trust in and being disappointed. It wasn't long after Moses led them to a great victory that they began to grumble about his abilities.

I think we can all probably relate to this situation, and I am sure at one point in your life just as in mine you have chosen to follow a leader only to be disappointed.

Even in their grumblings the Lord provided for them and gave them sweet water to drink. I wonder how often the Lord blesses us in our grumblings when we least deserve it?

Ultimately, the Lord gave them the answer and that is to focus on the Lord and not the man leading them. If we keep our focus on Him instead of the man, He will provide for us above and beyond what we expect. He will bring us out of Egypt and provide sweet waters to us.

Would you pray with me today: Lord, help me to not look to man for the answers. Help me to be thankful for the leaders you put into my life and help me to keep my eyes fixed on you and not them. Please let me experience the sweet waters today. Amen!

A Friend in Need

Exodus 17:8-16

8 The Amalekites came and attacked the Israelites at Rephidim. 9 Moses said to Joshua,"Choose some of our men and go out to fight the Amalekites. Tomorrow I will stand on top of the hill with the staff of God in my hands."

10 So Joshua fought the Amalekites as Moses had ordered, and Moses, Aaron and Hur went to the top of the hill. 11 As long as Moses held up his hands, the Israelites were winning,but whenever he lowered his hands, the Amalekites were winning. 12 When Moses' hands grew tired, they took a stone and put it under him and he sat on it. Aaron and Hur held his hands up—one on one side, one on the other—so that his hands remained steady till sunset. 13 So Joshua overcame the Amalekite army with the sword.

14 Then the LORD said to Moses, "Write this on a scroll as something to be remembered and make sure that Joshua hears it, because I will

completely blot out the name of Amalek from under heaven."

15 Moses built an altar and called it "The LORD is my Banner". 16 He said, "Because hands were lifted up against the throne of the LORD, the LORD will be at war against the Amalekites from generation to generation."

Have you ever had anybody give you a word of encouragement just when you needed it? I used to play sports, and wrestling was my favorite, but it required hard work and extreme effort. After all that effort I would sometimes get my butt kicked. It was very discouraging to say the least. One day after a few tough matches I remember is I practiced my coach came and said you are doing great and remember the cream always rises to the top. This encouraged me at a moment of weakness, at a moment of doubt. He lifted me up so that I would find the strength to fight.

Imagine how differently this battle would have ended up if Aaron and Hur didn't come along side Moses. What would have been the consequences on the battlefield if they didn't think of helping Moses?

So many times, in our Christian Walk we as men feel it necessary to fix the problem, correct the wrongs, even criticize. How might we affect the battle a brother is going through if we just came beside him and lifted his hands? Have you encouraged anyone lately? Have you spoken a kind word to a brother? This week may be your opportunity to lift up the hands of someone to help them win a battle.

Would you pray this prayer today? Lord help me to be encourager today and not a criticizer. Help me to build up my brothers and family today. Please Lord give me an opportunity to speak a word of kindness into someone's life today. Thank you, Lord! Amen

Hunger

Ezekiel 3:1-3

3 And he said to me, "Son of man, eat whatever you find here. Eat this scroll, and go, speak to the house of Israel." [2] So I opened my mouth, and he gave me this scroll to eat. [3] And he said to me, "Son of man, feed your belly with this scroll that I give you and fill your stomach with it." Then I ate it, and it was in my mouth as sweet as honey.

I once went to one of Mario Batali's restaurants. For those of you that don't know he is a world-famous chef and has numerous shows on the Food Network. Anyways it was one of his stake houses and it was amazing. The meal was something like 8 or 9 courses. The food was so good I could not get enough and even though I was full I kept eating until my stomach was so full I couldn't eat anymore. If I could have just rested for an hour or two and then ate more, I would have done it. The food was just that good!

In the scripture above we find God telling Ezekiel to eat a scroll. This scroll contained the words that God wanted him to speak. So, Ezekiel obeyed God and ate it and found that it tasted very good. It was as sweet as honey! MMMM MMMM good!

Let me ask a question to all of us. What are you filling your stomach with?

There are lots of things to fill our appetite with. We as men sometimes settle for what is second best, maybe even third or fourth best! When we could be eating 16 oz. bone in ribeye's made by the master chef.

Don't fill your hunger with temporal things. Instead fill your belly with the Word of God.

The champion eaters train themselves by eating a lot so that their stomachs will expand, and they will be able to fit more in. Train yourselves to devour the Word of God. Expand your spiritual stomach and taste that is good! Find time alone in His word, find study groups to be involved in, get to Sunday school, and engage in the message on Sunday.

It is there in abundance for you and all you have to do is eat!

Will you pray with me today? Lord, give me a hunger for your Word. When I read your Word, please make it sweet as honey to me. Fill me with your goodness and an understanding that can only come from your Word. Draw me closer during those times of study. Thank you for giving us the eternal food and removing the temporal things. Amen

Boot Camp

Galatians 2:20

20 I have been crucified with Christ. It is no longer I who live, but Christ who lives in me. And the life I now live in the flesh I live by faith in the Son of God, who loved me and gave himself for me.

One of the main points of military boot camp is to break you down so that you can follow orders. You go with very little and then they shave your head and dress you the same. Your habits and routines are broken and replaced with new military habits and routines. At the end the old you who once did what he wanted when he wanted now follows orders with discipline and skill. You have truly given your life to a cause that you believe in. The colors of your country's flag flows through your blood!

What would it take to live totally committed to Christ? How would that person look? Why would one do that?

Well, you would have to break down in some way to start with. You would have to be willing to put that old self, habits, and routines to death. In Roman times crucifixion was not only a way of putting someone to death but it was a way of torture, a way to inflict severe pain, a way to ensure the subject of punishment did not live. I have heard it said that A.W. Tozer said there was one thing you knew about a man carrying a cross out of town that he wasn't coming back!

Are you willing to be broken down to put that old self to death? Are you willing to be crucified today? It may require God to send you through a boot camp of His own making which will ensure a piece of you dies today and it no longer you who live but Christ who lives in me!

Will you pray with me today? Lord, take all of me today! Show me the things I need to crucify. Help me to take them to the cross and make through the suffering of dealing with these things. Break me down so that I may follow your commands and live by faith in the one who loved me and gave Himself for me. Amen!

Grappling!

Genesis 32:22-32

***22 The same night he arose and took
his two wives, his two female
servants, and his eleven
children, and crossed the ford of
the Jabbok. 23 He took them and sent
them across the stream, and
everything else that he had. 24 And
Jacob was left alone. And a man
wrestled with him until the breaking
of the day.25 When the man saw that
he did not prevail against Jacob, he
touched his hip socket, and Jacob's
hip was put out of joint as he
wrestled with him. 26 Then he said,
"Let me go, for the day has broken."
But Jacob said, "I will not let you go
unless you bless me." 27 And he said
to him, "What is your name?" And he
said, "Jacob." 28 Then he said, "Your
name shall no longer be called
Jacob, but Israel, for you have
striven with God and with men, and
have prevailed." 29 Then Jacob asked
him, "Please tell me your name." But***

he said, "Why is it that you ask my
name?" And there he blessed
him. 30 So Jacob called the name of
the place Peniel, saying, "For I have
seen God face to face, and yet my
life has been delivered." 31 The sun
rose upon him as he passed Penuel,
limping because of his
hip. 32 Therefore to this day the
people of Israel do not eat the sinew
of the thigh that is on the hip socket,
because he touched the socket of
Jacob's hip on the sinew of the
thigh.

I heard it said once that college wrestlers can lose up to 12 pounds in one match from the shear exertion. Wrestling is a hard sport and is just you and the other man. It takes skill, strength, and endurance amongst many other things to compete in wrestling. When you run into someone equally skilled or greater than you the amount of effort it takes is enormous. You fight for every little inch of space and battle until one man either makes a mistake or the other gives in from exhaustion.

Don't you find when you wrestle with God you end up pretty exhausted?

Usually, we wrestle with the Lord over something He wants us to do, and we are not willing. We wonder why things are not going our way and why we feel tired. The Lord is a much better wrestler than us. He has the strength, skill, and endurance to win out every time.

What are you wrestling with the Lord about today? Just give in and submit to Him and you will save yourself a lot of energy and headache. The Lords plan for your life is much better than your plan. Stop wrestling with the champ and know just like Jacob did that your life has been delivered.

Will you pray with me today? Lord help me to give up myself and the things I am holding onto. Please help me to see what I am wrestling with you for and what I need to let go of. May have the strength today to lay down that thing I am holding onto. Amen

Cultivation

Hebrews 6:7-8

[7] For land that has drunk the rain that often falls on it and produces a crop useful to those for whose sake it is cultivated, receives a blessing from God. [8] But if it bears thorns and thistles, it is worthless and near to being cursed, and its end is to be burned.

Much of California is currently under a drought. The drought has been going on for years. Right now, the farms are getting some water but if it keeps going at the rate it is going there won't be any water left. The land will suck all the water dry and it will not be able to be cultivated any more. Once land dries up nothing of usefulness can grow there and ultimately it stops producing crops and becomes worthless. Leaving the land like this in such a sunny climate allows it to burn and crack in the sun.

Let me ask a question, are you drinking in the rain?

Today many profess to be Christian but nothing of God is being cultivated in their lives. Their lives are not producing a crop. These types of professing Christians do not attend church regularly, do not have a hunger for the Word, and their prayer life is non-existent.

If you are one who drinks up the blessings of the Lord, you will have signs in your life that you are being cultivated. Not that everything will be easy, but you will be producing a crop. You'll want to attend church and other gatherings of the saints. You'll love the word of God and not be able to get enough of it and most certainly you will always find time to spend in prayer with the Father.

It is hard work to farm and cultivate land. Just like it is hard work to cultivate your spiritual life in a world like today's. On a farm you must plow the land and run irrigation to make things grow. In your spiritual life you must work the land too. You can do this by digging into the word of God and studying it and by spending time in prayer getting to know the will of the Father.

As you plow the land of your own life you will see the crops begin to grow. If you are in a drought, it is not too late for you to drink up some of the rains the Lord has for your life. Let today be the day you begin to grow them crops.

Let us pray today. Lord, help me to not be dry. Help me to drink up the rain of your Spirit in my life today. Help me to plow those fields that need plowing. Please send a fresh rain of you Spirit into my life today. Amen!

Eye Protection

Isaiah 6:1-5

***In the year that King Uzziah died
I saw the Lord sitting upon a throne,
high and lifted up; and the train[a] of
his robe filled the temple. 2 Above
him stood the seraphim. Each
had six wings: with two he covered
his face, and with two he covered his
feet, and with two he flew. 3 And one
called to another and said:***

***"Holy, holy, holy is the Lord of hosts;
the whole earth is full of his glory!"***

***4 And the foundations of the
thresholds shook at the voice of him
who called, and the house was filled
with smoke. 5 And I said: "Woe is
me! For I am lost; for I am a man of
unclean lips, and I dwell in the midst
of a people of unclean lips; for my
eyes have seen the King, the Lord of
hosts!"***

You can't look at a solar eclipse directly even with regular sunglasses because your eyes will take in too much ultraviolet radiation. If you do look at the eclipse without proper equipment you take a chance of damaging your retinas. Although, a solar eclipse is very tempting to see because it is such a phenomenon it is not recommended to do.

Many believers say I can't wait until the Lord comes back. What a glorious day that will be!

Oh, but how will we stand in His presence? Will we not be just like Isaiah crying out "woe is me?" There is nothing that will be left secret at that moment when the Lord returns. Just like a solar eclipse could burn your eyes, the glory of the Lord will burn away your sin. The more we realize the uncleanness of our hearts and minds the more the Lord will cleanse us. The more the Lord will consume us in a burning fire.

So today ask the Lord to show you a bit of Himself so that you may see what must be cleaned in your lives. It may be your lips need cleaned or your eyes or maybe even your heart. Whatever it is that needs cleaned, a glimpse at the Holy Lord will change you forever.

Let's pray today. Lord, please allow me to see enough of You to change my heart today. Allow me to see Your holiness for with no special lenses and burn the sin away from my life. Free me and save me from a people of unclean lips. Help me to be more like Christ today by gaining a glimpse of your holiness. Amen

Change the View

Jeremiah 1:5

"Before I formed you in the womb I knew you,
and before you were born I consecrated you;
I appointed you a prophet to the nations."

My son loves Legos! He especially loves the kits that build a guy. He gets excited whenever he gets a new kit because he knows if he follows the instructions at the end the figure on the box will be created.

I find a great sense of accomplishment when I build something. At the end of the building process there is a new chair, TV stand, or whatever it maybe. The fruit of my labor has yielded a result.

God created you and designed you to His specification. He knew your personality strengths and flaws. He knew how those things would be affected by your circumstances while growing old and when you choose to follow Him, He looks at you with a great sense of accomplishment.

You are the fruit of His suffering, the reward for His effort. Not that God needs encouragement like you or me but that the creator of the universe takes joy in you when you follow Christ.

Do you believe God is well pleased with you at this very moment? Do you believe that He sees you as a Holy being?

Well, He does! He doesn't look at you through your eyes or my eyes once you make that decision to live for Christ. Oh no, He looks at you through the blood-stained eyes of Christ. Through the blood that has washed your sins as white as snow!

So today I challenge you as a believer in Christ to live the life the Creator of the universe appointed you to. Live for Him today.

Will you pray with me? Lord, I have such a hard time believing you view me this way. Please help me to see myself the way you see me. Give me the eyes to see the truth. Help me to believe I am the fruit of your suffering and labor. Thank you Lord that you view me this in these ways and knew me in my mother's womb. Amen!

May you see the truth about the way God views you today!

Heavenly Results

Jeremiah 1:4-10

4 Then the word of the LORD came to me, saying:

5 "Before I formed you in the womb I knew you;
Before you were born I sanctified you;
I ordained you a prophet to the nations."

6 Then said I:

"Ah, Lord GOD!
Behold, I cannot speak, for I *am* a youth."

7 But the LORD said to me:

"Do not say, 'I *am* a youth,'
For you shall go to all to whom I send you,
And whatever I command you, you shall speak.
8 Do not be afraid of their faces,

For I *am* with you to deliver you," says the LORD.

9 Then the LORD put forth His hand and touched my mouth, and the LORD said to me:

"Behold, I have put My words in your mouth.
10 See, I have this day set you over the nations and over the kingdoms,
To root out and to pull down,
To destroy and to throw down,
To build and to plant."

David Wilkerson wrote the following about George Bowen a missionary to India:

One of the great missionaries to have impacted my life is George Bowen. His life was a powerful example, and his book, Love Revealed, is one of the greatest books on Christ I've ever read. A single man, Bowen turned away from wealth and fame to become a missionary in Bombay, India, in the mid-1800s.

When he saw the missionaries there living well above the poor they ministered to, Bowen gave up his mission support and chose to live among the very poorest. He dressed as the Indians did, and embraced poverty, living in a humble dwelling and subsisting sometimes only on bread and water. He preached on the streets in sweltering weather, distributing gospel literature and weeping over the lost.

This amazingly devoted man had gone to India with high hopes for the ministry of the gospel. And he'd given everything toward that end, his heart, mind, body and spirit. Yet, in his forty-plus years of ministry in India, Bowen had not one convert. It was only after his death that mission societies discovered he was one of the most beloved missionaries in the nation. Even heathen idol-worshipers looked to Bowen as the example of what a Christian is.

Today, George Bowen's humble life and powerful words still enflame my soul and the souls of others worldwide.

Could you do it? Could you serve like Jeremiah or George Bowen? Spend your entire life doing what living for Christ, speaking the words He gave you, ministering, witnessing day after day, all for not one single convert. Could you do it?

By today's standards these men are utter failures. Jeremiah was a prophet and no one listened to him. He suffered numerous times for giving his message and ultimately saw the destruction of the place he called home and his friends and neighbors carried off to captivity or killed.

George Bowen gave up all the comforts of missionary funding of the time to move to the slums and live in poverty while he ministered day after day for over 40 years and not one convert. Not one single person coming to faith in Christ! He was supposed to be a missionary and he failed according to the job description.

So could you do it? Better yet can you do it now? Can you surrender your life completely to Christ and risk being a complete failure in the world's eyes for the sake of the kingdom?

It is understandable that we want to see results. I am sure I am not the only one who loves to know they have been used by God. It makes you feel good but realistically in our culture most of the time it is rejection and failure. These are not what God feels toward us but rather how the world thinks of it. For those of us who are believers in Christ we know it is not about statistics, buildings, ministry size, but rather about our faith in Christ.

For most of us we will probably never know the impact we have had on this world until we are in glory. So don't worry about the results or what the world says is a success. Just keep on living for the One who loves you and guides your steps and when you get there I am sure you will hear "Well done good and faithful servant."

Let's pray. Oh Lord, help me to not be discouraged by the results. Help me to be thankful that You have chosen me as one of Your representatives to this messed up world. Help me to live like Christ today. Help to share your grace and love with those around me today. Thank you for all you have done in my life and all you are going to do. Amen

Designer

Jeremiah 33:1-3

33 The word of the LORD came to Jeremiah a second time, while he was still shut up in the court of the guard: 2 "Thus says the LORD who made the earth, the LORD who formed it to establish it—the LORD is his name: 3 Call to me and I will answer you, and will tell you great and hidden things that you have not known.

I work on computers and I am now an engineer but it wasn't always this way. I started at the bottom with very little knowledge. I could install Windows and hook up a PC which was the extent of my knowledge. Over time I learned there was so much more to the computer than the operating system. I learned this from people who knew more than me. I learned from people who had designed the networks and the infrastructure that ran the businesses.

Is there a better way to get an answer than going to the designer? If I wanted to know what wire needed to be plugged in to what port in order to make a computer talk to the rest of them, I would read the diagram created by the network designer. When I followed the instructions, everything would work, and I would gain understanding of the network.

I believe some of us and maybe all of us have experienced trouble like Jeremiah. We feel shut up or a better way to put it in prison. We look around the world and see no answers. We see what seems like evil winning. We may even see that in our own lives! Sin can and will make us feel shut in and all alone. We can often wonder how we get victory in the battle. Some of us are facing small battles and others reading this are fighting for their very lives.

I believe this is not only a promise for Jeremiah but a promise for all of us today at this very moment. Go to the designer, the Lord who made the earth and all that is in it. Call to Him who created you and He promises to answer you and show you great and hidden things. Ask Him to show the reasons why you are stuck in that sin. Ask Him to show you what it is that you have buried deep inside you that causes you to act the way you do. Ask Him to show you the pain you are bearing.

I believe He will show you and reveal to you the answers to these questions. He will reveal the plan for the greatness He has in store for you. As this chapter goes on, the Lord promises to bring life in abundance to a place that has been laid to waste. This is His plan for you! He wants to reveal great things to you and bring them forth in your life in that place of desolation. There is hope, there is promise, and it will come to be.

Will you pray with me today? Lord search me! Show me the things in my life that cause my attitudes, my hurts, and my sin. Reveal to me the great plan you have for my life. Thank you, Lord, for what you are about to do. Amen

Burnt Offerings

Job 1:5

[5] And when the days of the feast had run their course, Job would send and consecrate them, and he would rise early in the morning and offer burnt offerings according to the number of them all. For Job said, "It may be that my children have sinned, and cursed[a] God in their hearts." Thus Job did continually.

With any sport you must practice something over and over again for it to take effect. For a team to move in unison they must drill the plays over and over again and if one is out of step the whole team is out of step. You must coach to that weakest link to make them strong because your unit or team will never get it right if there is one out of place. They will look awkward, or their play will not flow right. It is the coaches' job to ensure they continue to practice this and work to get it right.

Job's children liked to party and have a good time. The children chose to live their lives their way and not the way of their father. They continued to practice things that were not good. So, Job did what any good father would do he would offer burnt offerings for each of his children continually in hopes that they might be saved.

Oh, how many of us know this story all too well. The loved ones who go on about their business each day with no thought of Christ and what He has done for us. Yet, we pray for them with the hope that they might be saved. We pray they would come to knowledge of Christ on this very day. We continue to offer up our burnt offerings according to the number of them all just as Job did. We must continue this for their sake. We must continue to practice to ensure they end up on the right team.

Let us pray today. Lord, you know I love my lost loved ones and I pray for their salvation. Lord, please break through to their hearts today. Let today be the day of their salvation. Would you please come and meet them where they're today? I pray all of this in your holy and precious name Jesus! Amen

Rejects

John 1:9-13

**9 There was the true Light which,
coming into the world, enlightens
every man. 10 He was in the world,
and the world was made through
Him, and the world did not know
Him. 11 He came to His own, and
those who were His own did not
receive Him. 12 But as many as
received Him, to them He gave the
right to become children of God,
even to those who believe in His
name, 13 who were born, not of
blood nor of the will of the flesh nor
of the will of man, but of God.**

There are some people out there that have been rejected many times in their lives. Some who have been rejected by their families for things they have done or things they didn't do. There are some who have been rejected by friends because they wouldn't go with the crowd or maybe just because they were not needed anymore. There are some who have been rejected because they were a stepchild and not blood. Then there are those who are rejected by society because they are different, weak, poor, or you name it. This world is harsh, and rejection happens all the time.

Think of being a child and being told you will never be good enough or amount to anything continually throughout your youth. Think of being an ex-con for doing something stupid and no one giving you a second chance. Think of doing your job better than everyone but continually getting passed over because you are not in tight with the boss or better yet not willing to do wrong to advance someone's agenda. The list goes on and on!

This verse tells us Christ came to His own, to the people God had chosen to represent Him from the beginning of time and they rejected Him. In fact, they killed Him because they didn't want Him and yet the greatest evil man could ever do God used for the greatest good in the universe. He used it to save those who have been rejected, those who have been given up on, and those who are forgotten.

God has chosen to give you who believe in Christ the right to become His child! Yes, that is you no matter what your faults or failures are! He chose you no matter what your income is or the color of your skin. He chose you and He understands what rejection has made you feel, and He can heal those hurts and conquer those fears. He will do it because you are part of His family now. You are a child of God!

You who believe are no longer born of this world, blood, or flesh. You are born of greatness, victory, hope, healing, and all the good you could ever name. You who are born again are born of God and will never reject you, leave you or forsake you!

Let us pray today. Oh Father God, heal the wounds of my past and make me whole. Mend the brokenness in my life. Let me experience your great love for me today like I have never experienced before. Help me to know I am not rejected but rather that I am received as a child into the family of God. Thank you Lord! Amen.

Commandment Issues

John 3:1-17

3 There was a man of the Pharisees
named Nicodemus, a ruler of the
Jews. 2 This man came to Jesus by
night and said to Him, "Rabbi, we
know that You are a teacher come
from God; for no one can do these
signs that You do unless God is with
him."

3 Jesus answered and said to
him, "Most assuredly, I say to you,
unless one is born again, he cannot
see the kingdom of God."

4 Nicodemus said to Him, "How can a
man be born when he is old? Can he
enter a second time into his
mother's womb and be born?"

5 Jesus answered, "Most assuredly, I
say to you, unless one is born of
water and the Spirit, he cannot enter
the kingdom of God. 6 That which is
born of the flesh is flesh, and that

which is born of the Spirit is
spirit. 7 Do not marvel that I said to
you, 'You must be born again.' 8 The
wind blows where it wishes, and you
hear the sound of it, but cannot tell
where it comes from and where it
goes. So is everyone who is born of
the Spirit."

9 Nicodemus answered and said to
Him, "How can these things be?"

10 Jesus answered and said to
him, "Are you the teacher of Israel,
and do not know these
things? 11 Most assuredly, I say to
you, we speak what We know and
testify what We have seen, and you
do not receive Our witness. 12 If I
have told you earthly things and you
do not believe, how will you believe
if I tell you heavenly things? 13 No
one has ascended to heaven but He
who came down from heaven, *that*
***is,* the Son of Man who is in**
heaven.[a] 14 And as Moses lifted up
the serpent in the wilderness, even

so must the Son of Man be lifted up,[15] that whoever believes in Him should not perish but[b] have eternal life. [16] For God so loved the world that He gave His only begotten Son, that whoever believes in Him should not perish but have everlasting life. [17] For God did not send His Son into the world to condemn the world, but that the world through Him might be saved.

Did you know that humanists have a set of ten commandments? In their very hate of God, they cannot get away from the fact that we need to be governed by something but that is a different message for a different day. Did you know we Christians have **THE** Ten Commandments? They are the law governs all things written by the very finger of God on stone and given to us I am sure you who believe knew this. So please, excuse my sarcasm.

So let me say this, just obey! Just be obedient to the Word of God! That's it! Just do that and everything will be great. Go ahead.

So, know that we got that out of the way let me ask you how are you doing at being obedient today? Is this your relationship with God?

If I had a dollar for every time I heard it is a matter of obedience, I would be a wealthy man and I understand it is easy to come to this conclusion. Certainly, we should do as the Lord says but is obedience really the key?

Nicodemus who this passage tells us was a Pharisee comes to talk with Jesus. During the conversation Jesus tells this man that he must be born again. Jesus tells him he must be born of the Spirit and maybe Nicodemus is not the smartest Pharisee or maybe his years of studying the scripture, going to temple, and trying to be obedient to every letter of the law have warped his thinking because he ask Jesus how can this be?

Why would Jesus tell a Pharisee who lived their lives with a pursuit of holiness and knowledge of the scriptures that would put even the greatest theologians, preachers, and professing believers of today to shame? Why doesn't Jesus just tell him to be obedient?

I can't do it no matter how hard I try to; I can't be 100% obedient to God. I fail every time I try to do it on my own. When I think I shouldn't do this because it is not very Christian, or I know this as against God's law. I can bear the burden for only so long and then I collapse under the weight of the law. Maybe I am all alone in this and everyone reading this never sins, but I don't think that's true.

So, I ask again is it about obedience?

If it were the world would be a much better place because the humanist knows that it's not right to lie, steal, kill, covet, etc.... but in all of man's strength we can't do it.

I believe it is about much more than obedience, the law, or my knowledge on the subject. It is about surrender. It is about surrender unto death. As the scriptures say, unless that grain of wheat falls to the ground and dies it will not produce. When that grain falls on the ground dead it begins to grow again, and I guess you could say it is born again.

Are you born again today? Are you born of the Spirit? Or are you born of a system of beliefs that you are trying to be obedient to?

Join me today and stop trying to do it on your own. Surrender to the will of God and be born of the Spirt. Then you will find obedience flows from through you.

Cry out with me today. Lord, please baptize me in your Spirit. Help me to not do it out of my strength or abilities. Help to surrender all I have to You. Lord, change me! Lord, save me from myself and fill me with your Spirit. Amen.

Don’t Give Up

Luke 8:49-56

49 While he was still speaking,
someone from the ruler's house
came and said, "Your daughter is
dead; do not trouble the Teacher
anymore." 50 But Jesus on hearing
this answered him, "Do not fear;
only believe, and she will be
well."51 And when he came to the
house, he allowed no one to enter
with him, except Peter and John and
James, and the father and mother of
the child. 52 And all were weeping
and mourning for her, but
he said, "Do not weep, for she is not
dead but sleeping." 53 And they
laughed at him, knowing that she
was dead.54 But taking her by the
hand he called,
saying, "Child, arise." 55 And her
spirit returned, and she got up at
once. And he directed that
something should be given her to
eat. 56 And her parents were amazed,

but he charged them to tell no one what had happened.

I remember as a teen I decided to run for student council president. I went to get the signatures necessary to run and got my name on the ballot. Once I had my name in the running, I received very little votes and most people laughed at me for even trying and said you were serious? This left a lot of doubt in pain in my mind.

Imagine the doubt that crept into Jairus heart and mind as he heard the people mock and laugh at Jesus words "Do not weep, for she is not dead but sleeping."?

Do we do this with the Lord? How often do we just give up on going to the Lord because He hasn't answered our prayers right away? How do we feel when we get the bad news and tell people we are going to pray about it only to be laughed at and told pray if you want?

This all leads to deep hurts and a weakening of our faith but in two words Jesus' change everything "Child, arise."

With two words God can change our lives and answer whatever it is you are praying for on this day. Hold strong friends and do not give up the faith. God will answer and you will be amazed!

Let's give Him praise today. Lord, we praise your holy name for it has the power to heal the sick and bring salvation to the lost. We praise you for all you have done in our lives and all you are about to do. Amen

Right View

Luke 9:51-56

***51 Now it came to pass, when the
time had come for Him to be
received up, that He steadfastly set
His face to go to Jerusalem, 52 and
sent messengers before His face.
And as they went, they entered a
village of the Samaritans, to prepare
for Him. 53 But they did not receive
Him, because His face was set for
the journey to Jerusalem. 54 And
when His disciples James and John
saw this, they said, "Lord, do You
want us to command fire to come
down from heaven and consume
them, just as Elijah did?"***

***55 But He turned and rebuked
them, and said, "You do not know
what manner of spirit you are
of. 56 For the Son of Man did not
come to destroy men's lives but to
save them." And they went to
another village.***

It's election time. We have primaries and caucuses going on and candidates are trying to convince us they are the right choice to lead us to a better future. Maybe I dare say they are even trying to convince us they are the ones to save the country from the dangers ahead. All the while we will vote for the one, we think does best and based on what we think we know about the man or woman. We form an opinion of how they will lead us without ever really knowing them at all.

Here in these verses Jesus has made His mind up that it was time to go to Jerusalem and complete the task for which He had come. We see that James and John had an idea of what kind of savior He was to be and when He was rejected, they wanted to use power to teach the Samaritans a lesson, but Jesus strongly corrects them by telling them just what kind of savior He is and that he is not here to destroy but save.

You see James and John didn't have bad intentions. After all they just wanted people to respect Christ, but their view of Jesus was misguided. They were expecting a messiah to take the world by force and change their situation in a worldly way.

Let me ask today what is your view of the Messiah? Is it a view that He is here to change the world by force? Or is it a view that He is here to change the hearts of men and women? Do you really believe that Christ is the savior of mankind and that His sacrifice and resurrection are the example and answer to all the problems of the heart? Do you believe He can reach all men from lowest of the low to the mightiest of men?

I ask you today are you just professing to know the Christ from snippets you have heard and actions of others or do you really know the savior that has come to save?

Would you pray with me today? Dear Lord, I pray with all my might, all my strength, and whatever faith I have that you make yourself more known to me today. I pray that you help me get the right view of what you are doing in my life and the world around me. Amen!

Save Them

Luke 16:19-31

**19 "Now there was a rich man, and he
habitually dressed in purple and fine
linen, joyously living in splendor
every day. 20 And a poor man named
Lazarus was laid at his gate, covered
with sores, 21 and longing to be fed
with the *crumbs* which were falling
from the rich man's table; besides,
even the dogs were coming and
licking his sores. 22 Now the poor
man died and was carried away by
the angels to Abraham's bosom; and
the rich man also died and was
buried. 23 In Hades he lifted up his
eyes, being in torment and saw
Abraham far away and Lazarus in his
bosom. 24 And he cried out and said,
'Father Abraham, have mercy on me,
and send Lazarus so that he may dip
the tip of his finger in water and cool
off my tongue, for I am in agony
in this flame.' 25 But Abraham said,**

**'Child, remember that during your
life you received your good things,
and likewise Lazarus bad things; but
now he is being comforted here, and
you are in agony. 26 And besides all
this, between us and you there is a
great chasm fixed, so that those who
wish to come over from here to you
will not be able, and *that* none may
cross over from there to us.' 27 And
he said, 'Then I beg you, father, that
you send him to my father's house—
28 for I have five brothers—in order
that he may warn them, so that they
will not also come to this place of
torment.' 29 But Abraham said, 'They
have Moses and the Prophets; let
them hear them.' 30 But he said,
'No, father Abraham, but if someone
goes to them from the dead, they
will repent!' 31 But he said to him, 'If
they do not listen to Moses and the
Prophets, they will not be persuaded
even if someone rises from the
dead.'"**

Those of us who have kids know what it is like to tell a child "Don't do that because you can get hurt" and inevitably they continue to do it anyways until they get hurt. Then they look at you like, "why did you let me do that! They just don't believe you until they have experienced the consequence for their actions. You love that child, and you do everything to warn them about the dangers and try to help them avoid the consequence but they are human after all and everyone knows what it is like to not heed the warnings!

Anyone reading this has probably experienced something like I was just talking about in their lives. They had someone warn them about something, but you just couldn't help yourself, or maybe you just didn't want to listen, or maybe you just didn't believe the consequence would be that bad.

Having read all that, I'm sure you are thinking the next thing is going to be if we do bad and don't follow Jesus we are going to hell, and this is why we should believe in Christ. While that all may be true that is not why hell is talked about so much in the Bible.

If you are witnessing to someone and trying to get them to come to Christ so they can avoid eternal damnation, it's probably not going so good and if you came to faith for that reason then you know what I am talking about. This causes two things in people fear and legalism and neither are something Christ has for you.

2nd Timothy 1:7 says the following "[7] **For God has not given us a spirit of fear, but of power and of love and of a sound mind."** Living in fear is not what God wants from you and fear is not from God! He has loves you more than anything and God wants you to know this more than anything else in the universe. God loves you! Do not be afraid!

If we live in fear, we try to obey God out of fear of condemnation and then we really are not free, but rather we are then still in bondage to the law. When you know someone loves you, your natural inclination is to love them back. You don't worry that nothing you do will be good enough or that they are going to condemn you because that is not love.

The other reason hell is talked about is not to condemn us but to stir up are hearts for prayer for those who don't know the love of Christ! For those who don't know what it means to have a Father in Heaven who loves them! Ravi Zacharias quoted someone who said the only person they would listen to preach a message on hell was D.L. Moody because halfway through he would break down in tears.

Yes, the consequences of not following Christ are great and as one who knows the love of Christ and what people are missing you can't help but have the thought of people you care about and even people you don't know going to eternal damnation. So, cry out to God for this dying world and those who live in it! Get on your knees and weep for them to the Father who loves you and loves them!

Let's pray today. Oh Lord, Save them please! Save not just my family, but my co-workers, my friends, their friends. Save those who do evil Lord. Turn their hearts to You. Oh Please Lord, come down on this land today! Let me not be afraid but know that you are a God who has set me free to pray for others and show that love that you have shown me. So, that I might be part of you work today! Amen

Feed that Seed

Mark 4:3-9

3 "Listen! Behold, a Sower went out
to sow. 4 And as he sowed, some
seed fell along the path, and the
birds came and devoured it. 5 Other
seed fell on rocky ground, where it
did not have much soil, and
immediately it sprang up, since it
had no depth of soil. 6 And when the
sun rose, it was scorched, and since
it had no root, it withered
away. 7 Other seed fell
among thorns, and the thorns grew
up and choked it, and it yielded no
grain. 8 And other seeds fell into
good soil and produced grain,
growing up and increasing and
yielding thirtyfold and sixtyfold
and a hundredfold." 9 And he
said, "He who has ears to hear, let
him hear.

Have you ever walked through the woods where there are a lot of rocks in trees? You will sometimes see a tree growing out of a rock or a full-grown tree that's roots have overtaken the rock. It is now just as big as the other trees and its roots wrap around the rock down into the ground.

Quite literally the rock has been overtaken by the tree!

So many times, we look at the surroundings and say nothing can grow there. Why even sow seed in this place it appears hard but even some seed that is sown on rocky soil can overcome if it is nurtured and watered enough.

Do you have anyone that you want to come to the kingdom with you who is living in rocky soil? Do you feel like they will never be able to take root?

Sow that seed and feed it, water it, nurture it, until the seed is fully grown. You can help them to split the rock and dig their roots down deep. This can be done by walking beside them in the difficult times, by praying with them, and by helping them study the word of God. If we are willing to work the land it will produce a harvest. Never give up just because the soil looks hard!

Let us pray today. Lord, help me to see beyond the circumstances. Help me to see all things are possible with you. Help me to water, feed, and nurture the seeds I have sown. Show me where the ones that are ready fcr harvest are at! Give me the words and actions to sow for your kingdom. Amen!

Wisdom

Matthew 14:28-30

[28] For which of you, desiring to build a tower, does not first sit down and count the cost, whether he has enough to complete it? [29] Otherwise, when he has laid a foundation and is not able to finish, all who see it begin to mock him, [30] saying, 'This man began to build and was not able to finish.'

One day I got an idea to remodel the basement of my house. I was going to start with a bathroom and build out from there so my father-in-law could move in. I began by getting a general idea of what I needed but not an exact list or plan of what would be needed to complete the project. Well needless to say I got further into the project I realized I did not have any clue how I was going to finish. I was so far off that when I asked the neighbor to come take a look, he just laughed at the mess I was in.

How often do we do the same with spiritual things? We come up with an idea and say it's from God and decided to move forward in our own strength. We don't even commit any of it to prayer and if we do it is only for a short period. We choose not to think of the spiritual resistance we will face as we try to move forward. Plain and simple we would rather be doers of the word than hearers.

If I just would have done my research and reached out to some plumbers, I would have had a much better idea of what I was about to get into.

We have the word of God to guide us and those who have walked before us who are much more spiritually mature. They have wisdom given by God through years of walking in prayer and the Word. Seek them out and learn all you can from them! Don't look down on the older members of your congregation because they may be the very ones God has put in your life to help you count the cost and finish that which God has called you!

Would you pray with me today? Dear Lord, help me to find someone with wisdom and experience of walking faith out. Help me to learn from them before I run off on my own strength. Oh Lord, You alone know the plans for my life and I pray you help me to see them entirely and finish that which you wish to be built! Amen.

Do the Impossible

Nehemiah 2:17-18

[17] Then I said to them, "You see the trouble we are in, how Jerusalem lies in ruins with its gates burned. Come, let us build the wall of Jerusalem, that we may no longer suffer derision." [18] And I told them of the hand of my God that had been upon me for good, and also of the words that the king had spoken to me. And they said, "Let us rise up and build." So they strengthened their hands for the good work.

During World War II there was a German man who saw the evil that he was involved with and decided to save as many Jews as he could. This act was popularized in the movie Schindler's list based on the books about him. His actions saved 1,200 Jewish lives. One man in a very dark place made a difference.

Can one man make a difference in the world today?

Nehemiah saw his land in derision and suffering greatly. Everything that had been good had been destroyed or torn down but being a man of faith God put his hand on him for good.

Nehemiah was one man, but his faith and prayers gave him great strength. He encouraged his people through his faith to rise up and build. His abilities that were given from God were used to strengthen the hands of others and they were able to do good as well. Because of all these things Nehemiah was able to oversee the rebuilding of the wall in just 52 days. This was something that caused many to see what the power of faith through a man could accomplish.

Many have given up the fight today and they believe the lie from Satan that they cannot make a difference. Well with the Holy Spirit flowing through you, the very power of God can and will enable you to change the world around you.

Are there some walls in your life that need rebuilding? Has God shown these things, and you have shrunk back because you think it impossible? I encourage you to fear not and stand in faith. You by yourself with God flowing through you will strengthen the hands of others. You can do it!

Will you pray with me? Dear heavenly Father, show me the area where you want me to stand and impact the world. Please, show me the walls that need rebuilt around me. May your Spirit flow through me and help me to strengthen others. Amen!

May you do the impossible today.

Power in the Body

Proverbs 17:17

17 A friend loves at all times,
and a brother is born for a time of adversity.

The bonds of friendship run deep but the bonds of family run even deeper. People will defend their family even when they know their family is wrong.

If you go into the hood and try to steal from someone or hurt someone you will feel the wrath of the whole place. Even those who did not like each other an hour before will come together to drive you out. Why, you ask? Well, it is simple because they are bonded together by the adversity of life. They are a family born in a time of adversity.

Have you ever shared in adversity with someone?

If you have you know this verse to be true. There is something greater to be had than just friendship. Friends come and go but family stays forever.

This is why God views us is children. We are bonded together through the blood of Jesus Christ and His Holy Spirit which lives in us. The adversity we face when we proclaim Christ to the world or make decisions based on the Spirit guiding us and the Word of God unites us in a brotherhood, a sisterhood, a family bond that cannot be broken.

While we may not always see eye to eye it is when the enemy comes against one of our own that we come together to drive him out. We stand united in times of adversity as children of God.

Would you pray with me today? Dear Lord, please help me to experience this bond in a greater way with my Christian brothers and sisters. Help me to have a deeper relationship than just friendship. Build bonds of the Holy Spirit in my life and help me to see us as a family of God. Amen

Signs

Psalm 51:3-4

[3] For I know my transgressions,
and my sin is ever before me.
[4] Against you, you only, have I sinned
and done what is evil in your sight,
so that you may be justified in your words
and blameless in your judgment.

Many people put signs around their desk or office so that they might have a constant reminder of things. They may be little encouraging notes or inspirational pictures that remind them things are going to be better. They do these things to help take the focus off the negative things around them.

Do you have notes and signs constantly reminding you of your sin?

As psalmists wrote is your sin ever before you?

Many of us try to push this down and away with other reminders that we are good people, but the truth of the matter is we haven't just hurt others with our sin. No, we have sinned against a blameless God and He is gracious to put reminders there until we turn from it. He allows us to be reminded of our faults until we cry out to Him just is the psalmist did in this scripture ***"Create in me a clean heart, O God, and renew a right spirit within me."***

Once we come to this realization and need for Christ to transform us, He guarantees He will. At that moment all of your sin is blotted out and no longer counted against you. You are made holy in the sight of God. All it takes is repentance to be free and no longer held accountable for that sin. Christ has done enough to pay the price for that thing which is ever before you and now all you must do is accept it.

Will you accept it today?

Let us pray! Lord, I am sorry for my sins. Lord, please create in me a clean heart and renew a right spirit within me. Lord, fill me with your love and help me to see I am free from those things I repented of. Help me to believe that my repentance is enough. Thank you Jesus! Amen

Accusations Silenced

Revelation 12:10

10 And I heard a loud voice in heaven, saying, "Now the salvation and the power and the kingdom of our God and the authority of his Christ have come, for the accuser of our brothers[a] has been thrown down, who accuses them day and night before our God.

The story of Rubin "Hurricane" Carter was made famous by a Bob Dylan song. It is a story of a man who was wrongly accused and sentenced to prison because of those false accusations. Ultimately, because of people who believed in his innocence and those who fought for his freedom he was freed. It took twenty years, but he was free from the false accusations.

So many of us live with false accusations of guilt, shame, etc... or accusations that we are not free of our past. Every time we think free of an accusation the devil is there to whisper in our ear that we are still the same. The devil tries to convince us that Christ work was not good enough for our shame, our guilt, and our sins. The devil tries to convince us that if our brothers and sisters in Christ find out about our past, they will reject us. This is the enemy of our soul's pattern of operation. The devil only works in lies, fear, and accusations.

Well, this verse tells us what happens to the devil. He is thrown down because salvation and power have come to you through Christ! Victory is won and you are free of all the lies, fears, and accusations. When these tactics of Satan come to you can stand on the promise of Christ that you are free indeed! Walk in the freedom Christ has given you and tell the devil to go to hell where he belongs!

Will you pray with me today? Dear Lord, please show me the freedom I have in you. Show me freedom from past failures and hurts, the freedom from past lies and pains. Lord help me to walk in victory today! Amen

Hero

Romans 5:7-8

[7] For one will scarcely die for a righteous person—though perhaps for a good person one would dare even to die— [8] but God shows his love for us in that while we were still sinners, Christ died for us.

I could write so many things for an illustration here, but I am choosing not to. In all of our entertainment today there is an overriding theme of a need for a hero. We as a people are drawn to the idea of someone doing something extraordinary to defeat evil and save the day. Just think about it and put your own illustration here.

Sadly, we look to make believe heroes for relief from the evil in this world and in our own lives.

Today's devotional is a challenge to all men. I am asking you to think what in your life are you willing to die for?

Many I imagine would say family and some would even say close friends, but I am going to quote Leonard Ravenhill "Is what you are living for, worth Christ dying for?"

What would you do for a hero who saved your life from certain death? How would you honor the man who sacrificed himself to save you?

Would it be parades? Perhaps a memorial? Would you live like every day was your last? Would your life honor the hero?

We as a society look for a hero in every place and in every bad thing that occurs all while denying the one who saved us.

Today I encourage you as men of faith to lay down those things that are keeping you back from your Hero. I implore you to put those attitudes, actions, lust, and the lists goes on and on to death and glorify your Hero today.

We don't need Spiderman, Captain America, or any of the other make-believe heroes. We have the real deal, the one who wants to live in us so we can become heroes of faith with Him.

Would you pray with me today? Lord, I thank you for laying your life down for me when I didn't even know I was in danger. Thank you that I only need to look to you for an example of how to live. I pray that you help me to live as a hero of faith. I pray that you strengthen my walk of faith with you so that others will see you in me. Amen

Virus

Romans 5:13

12 Therefore, just as through one man sin entered into the world, and death through sin, and so death spread to all men, because all sinned

Everyone reading this has probably gotten the flu at some point in their life. Some of us have even gotten a really bad case of the flu. The kind of thing that causes pain and you start to wonder what I did to deserve this, but the truth is you did nothing. You just got sick and are feeling the effects of the illness.

Do you ever wonder what you did to deserve something in life? Why did I have to suffer as a child? Why did I lose that one I loved? Why am I losing my house? The list goes on and on. Maybe I am the only one, but I think we have all been there.

The truth is none of us asked for this sickness we have or to be affected by it. We all have a case of sin. It is who we are and what we desire. Go ahead and will yourself to not tell a lie and after years of not lying you will find out the pride you have in your hear when some ask you if you lie and you say no. It is our nature that passed to us from the beginning. We have to recognize the truth of this to receive the cure for our illness.

Only when you are willing to admit your sick can you take the cure.

Call on Christ today! Call on Him to cure you! Call on Him to make that which is disease ridden cleansed today!

He can and will change your life.

Will you pray with me today? Lord, I can't do this anymore. I try to be good on my own and change my ways, but I am a failure. Please change my heart, my attitudes, my desires, and my life. Amen!

Loyalty

Ruth 1:15-18

15 And she said, "See, your sister-in-law has gone back to her people and to her gods; return after your sister-in-law." 16 But Ruth said, "Do not urge me to leave you or to return from following you. For where you go I will go, and where you lodge I will lodge. Your people shall be my people, and your God my God. 17 Where you die I will die, and there will I be buried. May the LORD do so to me and more also if anything but death parts me from you." 18 And when Naomi saw that she was determined to go with her, she said no more.

My son has a dog. This dog sleeps with my son and sits with him every day. The dog gets excited to see my son when he comes home from school or if they have been apart. He is a cute little dog and we didn't think there was much fight in him or much of a protective side but when a stranger comes near my son or near the family the dog barks and stands his ground. This dog is loyal to the death for us!

Not to compare Ruth to a dog but her loyalty is amazing. She could have left Naomi behind for better things and chose to stay with her. She chose to suffer with her no matter what the cost even death.

Do we make the same choice today for Christ? Do we choose loyalty to the One who gave all for us? What sin are you putting over Christ today in your life? What friendship or material thing are you choosing over going where Christ wants you to go?

Let today be a new day in your life and go where Christ goes! Stay where the Lord stays! Make God's people your people! Then when you do these things you will know that not even death parts me from Christ the Lord of all!

Will you pray with me today? Thank you, Lord, that you paid it all for me! Thank you that I can go where you go, be where you be, and stay with your people! Help today to walk in this faith and stay strong in my belief. Help me to remain loyal to you over everything else in this world today! Amen.

Wounded Soldier

1 Peter 4:7-8

**7 The end of all things is at hand;
therefore, be self-controlled and
sober minded for the sake of your
prayers. 8 Above all, keep loving one
another earnestly, since love covers
a multitude of sins.**

You all probably have seen the image for the wounded warrior project but if you haven't let me describe it for you. It is a wounded soldier being carried on the back of a healthy soldier. I believe in the service there is a saying no man left behind!

The picture for the wounded warrior project speaks loudly about many things but when I read these verses and think about that picture, I am reminded it is the healthy soldier carrying the wounded man to safety.

Paul speaks about this often whether it is living to the measure you have attained or bearing one another burdens, but he always says to do it in love.

If you are like me, you probably have left a few soldiers on the battlefield. Maybe you are like me and even sent a few bullets their way instead of risking it all to carry them out.

I know this in a battle there is no time to discuss why the wounded got there or the folly of their decisions. No there is only how can we get them to safety so they can make it through.

So do is Peter says because the end may be near today for you or me or even all of us. KEEP LOVING one another earnestly and today might be the day you carry a wounded soldier to safety.

Let's pray! Thank you Lord that you have covered me so many times in my life. Thank you for all those who have covered me in my life. Help to be healthy today and to carry if I have too. Lord help me love rightly. Thank you for your mercy and grace. Amen!

Encouragement in the Daily

1 Thessalonians 5:11

11 Therefore encourage one another and build one another up, just as you are doing.

During a sports season a good coach will always find a way to help boost morale. The longevity and grind of practice almost always takes a toll on athletes. If the season is going well it takes an even greater toll. So, a coach must find a way to break routine. A good coach will build up rather than tear down. Encouragement goes a long way to success in athletics.

Many times, we feel like there must be more than this. You know the 9 to 5, the taking care of the kids, cleaning the house, going through the motions, and the list goes on and on. This ordinary life begins to drain us, and the same thing happens in our spiritual walk with Christ. It just becomes routine and then the whispers come in are you really living for the Lord at all.

As time goes on this leads to one thing guaranteed and that is DISCOURAGEMENT!

Well as Paul says here encourage one another and build one another up just as you are doing! I am willing to bet right now as some of you read this you are beginning to feel discouraged. Thinking I am not doing that at all.

Please be encouraged today because God sees your heart and all that you are doing. He sees the prayers you pray for your family, the work you do to provide, the house you clean, the church floor you sweep, the children you talk to, the pastor you say a kind word to, and the list goes on and on. You are being extraordinary in the ordinary. Every act you do out of the love of Christ in your heart is encouraging someone and building up the body and you may never see it.

Praise God for all you do today whether it be the greatest thing man has ever known or the smallest thing that no one ever knows. You are building up the kingdom.

Please pray with me. Lord, help me be encouraged today. Help me be an encouragement to others. Help me build those around me up rather than tear down. Help me to strengthen my family and those important to me. Help me encourage those I meet. Thank you for all you do Lord. May you help me be extraordinary in the ordinary today? Praise you and I love you! Amen!

Give it All

Colossians 3:23-24

23 Whatever you do, do your work heartily, as for the Lord rather than for men, 24 knowing that from the Lord you will receive the reward of the inheritance. It is the Lord Christ whom you serve

Vince Lombardi said the following "I firmly believe that any man's finest hour, the greatest fulfillment of all that he holds dear, is the moment when he has worked his heart out in a good cause and lies exhausted on the field of battle - victorious"

Football was different during his day. Men gave everything they had to the game. There were guys like Jack Youngblood whose team made it to the super bowl, but he broke his leg in the game before. So, he taped it up and played. Ronnie Lott broke his pinky finger in a game, and they told him he couldn't play anymore so he had the medical staff cut it off. The list goes on and on.

Now these are extreme examples, and I know that, but these men gave all in what they did. They were not made to be 9 to 5 guys they were football players who gave all to who they were supposed to be with no thought of the next game or season because today could be their last.

It would be easy for us to look at them and say we can't do that and get discouraged. I used to do the same in church. I'd look at the great saints around me and try to give an all to their standard. This ended in frustration every time.

We are not to give others all. We are to give to the measure we have today. You are not to give to the standard of Billy Graham or other great men of our time. You are to give your all in whatever measure you have attained. Remember this in all you do It is the Lord Christ whom you serve.

Live for Him today in whatever you do. Whether it be mowing the lawn, taking care of your family, doing the dishes, working on the job, and the list goes on!

At the end of the day may your head it the pillow exhausted from the field of battle – victorious in Him who has called you.

Let's pray! Dear Lord, please help me to give everything I got today. Please give me the strength to be the best in whatever responsibilities you have allowed me to have today. Lord, forgive me for in the past when I have only given you 2nd best. Help me today to be what you made to be today. Thank you, Lord! Amen

Walk On

Philippians 3:12-14

12 I don't mean to say that I have
already achieved these things or that
I have already reached perfection.
But I press on to possess that
perfection for which Christ Jesus
first possessed me. 13 No, dear
brothers and sisters, I have not
achieved it, but I focus on this one
thing: Forgetting the past and
looking forward to what lies
ahead, 14 I press on to reach the end
of the race and receive the heavenly
prize for which God, through Christ
Jesus, is calling us.

If you are like me, you there have probably been times in your life when you wish you could be like Doc Brown and Marty McFly and jump in the Delorian and blast back to the past to change the present. Well unfortunately that only works in the movies.

If we are all honest with ourselves there are certainly things we would like to go back in time and change but that is a regret and it's okay to wish for a do over. The problem is for most of us we hold onto the past and it defines us. This is not true in Christ.

This thing of not allowing our past to control us or define is exactly what Paul has realized and is sharing with the Philippians. He knows what he and all of us should be seeking Christ but isn't there yet but does not let a past in which his single mindedness blinded him from the truth of the Lord. The striving and mistakes of his life which include murder no longer define him Christ does.

Has Christ laid hold of you today? Do you believe your past is just that the past? Give it up to Him who has laid hold of you and look forward to what lies ahead. You are not who you were 10 years ago, 10 months ago or even 10 minutes ago. You belong to Christ today and is you press on with Him you will not be who your past says you are.

Praise God that when the Son sets your free you are free indeed.

Let's pray! Lord help me to realize I am not who my past says I am but who You say I am. Lord help me to live this very day for You and who You have made me to be. Thank you for all that you have brought me through and may my life glorify you today. Amen!

The Measure

Philippians 3:16-18

**15 Therefore let us, as many as are
mature, have this mind; and if in
anything you think otherwise, God
will reveal even this to
you.16 Nevertheless, to the
degree that we have already
attained, let us walk by the same
rule, let us be of the same mind.
17 Brethren, join in following my
example, and note those who so
walk, as you have us for a pattern**

In the early nineties there was a famous basketball player. You might have heard about him. His name was Michael Jordan. He was the best of that time and maybe even all the time. Because of his popularity a company put an ad out called be like Mike. The point of the ad was he was the best and we should try to be like him.

When I see this scripture, I can't help but think of be like Mike. How much time do we spend in our walk with Christ trying to be like someone else? Maybe I'm the only one who does this. You know look at someone and think wow they really know the Word, or they are a really good teacher. I need to be more like them.

So then if you are like me after thinking about this you set out to be like them. Which pretty much ends up in frustration because, as Paul says to the degree that we have already attained let us walk!

You may not have it all today, but you have something, and it is that measure that you need to live by. Don't try to be like Mike but rather be what Christ has made you to be on this day. Live for what Christ has revealed and is doing in your life today.

For those who believe in Christ He is making your life knew today to whatever measure you have attained. Walk with Him today and not the thought of what you should be.

Let's pray! Lord, I thank you for all you have done for me today. I thank you that I am not the same person I was years ago, months ago, or even yesterday. Please help me to live for what you have for me today. Help me to see the gifts you have blessed me with. Forgive me for the times when I tried to imitate others and not you. Thank you, Lord! Amen

Love More

Romans 12:9-10

[9] Let love be genuine. Abhor what is evil; hold fast to what is good.[10] Love one another with brotherly affection. Outdo one another in showing honor.

Everyone probably knows a guy who must one up everyone. If you caught a fish, he caught a bigger one. If you ran a race, he ran a faster one. The list goes on and on.   I think there is a little bit of this in all of us but some definitely more than others.

As I read these verses, I tried to think of another place the Bible tells us to one up on another but that's what it is saying here.

If you ever wanted to one up someone, do it in this way LOVE MORE! Show more honor to everyone around you than you deserve. Do this even if they don't deserve it. If you do this, you will be doing exactly what Paul speaks about so often. Loving and strengthening the body and this will be the time that out doing is actually a good thing.

So today when you have that chance humble yourself and take the extra step to honor someone, to love them, to hold fast to what is good, because it may be exactly the thing that someone needs.

Praise God for all He does for us!

Let's pray! Lord, please help me to love those around me today. Help me to show honor to everyone around me. Please help me to be a builder and not a destroyer. Thank you for all you do for me. Help me to glorify you today. Amen!

Today

James 4:14

[14] How do you know what your life will be like tomorrow? Your life is like the morning fog—it's here a little while, then it's gone. [15] What you ought to say is, "If the Lord wants us to, we will live and do this or that."

In gambling there is no such thing as a sure bet. There are ways to skew the odds in your favor and clever ways to cover those odds, but it is still called gambling for a reason. There is always an amount of uncertainty left to chance no matter how good you are. That's why it is a gamble. There is only one sure bet or investment in life and that is death. We are all guaranteed of this outcome. No one is getting out of here alive.

Last I checked this is an unarguable truth. So why do we spend so much time on tomorrow? And I guess another good question would be why do we spend so much time on yesterday as well?

This scripture reminds us that our life is just like a morning fog or vapor in other translations. It is here for a moment and gone in the next. We could waste what precious little time we have no regrets, worries, and fears but is that what the Lord wants?

Then we could waste on future plans, working ourselves to the bone to provide for tomorrow, saving every penny for retirement but is that what the Lord wants?

Today is the day you should live for! This does not mean throwing responsibility to the wayside but rather it means seeking Him just like the scripture says and ask Him what He has for you today. Give up all those concerns and burdens to the world and even the ones you put on yourself away and ask the Lord what He has for you today.

It is a gamble to ignore His will for you today and eternity with Him is not worth risking. Trust in Christ and let your past, present, and future belong to Him.

Please pray with me! Lord, please set me free from my worries and fears. Please free me from my need to control everything and help me to trust that Your plan is better than mine. Lord, help me to know that plan with all my heart today. Thank you that I'll get to spend eternity with you. I praise you and ask that I may glorify you today. Amen

Sliver of Light

John 1:5

The light shines in the darkness, and the darkness can never extinguish it.

In Johnny Cash's testimony he talks about a very dark moment in his life and how we wanted to commit suicide. So, he drove to some caves in his despair and climbed down as far is he could into the darkness hoping to get lost in it. The deeper he went the darker it got. Finally, he got to a point where there was nothing, but darkness and he sat down to die.

As he sat there, he talked to the Lord, and I can imagine the discussion. Why me
Lord? Why don't you just take me? You know the things you say to God when you are in the pit of despair. As he did this, he felt a sudden urge to live and to live for God but now he was so far into the caves with no light he didn't know how to get out and couldn't see the way home. He began to crawl and feel the

ground and cry out for help. At that moment he saw it. A beam of sunlight and is he kept moving toward the light and continued to grow and shine brighter until he was out of the darkness.

I am sure all of us have been there and some may be there now. We are stuck in the darkness of this world and even our own sin. We feel despair coming in on us and like we can't even see a sliver of light in our own life.

Well, keep crying out to the One who can save you. Call on the Christ for the light to shine into the darkness of your life and He will answer. Keep following that light even if it is only a sliver because no matter how hard the darkness tries around you it cannot extinguish that light.

Today is your day to shine brightly in a dark world. Ask Him who is able to fill you with the light to burn bright today.

Please pray with me! Lord, please fill me with your light. Give me more of the Holy Spirit than I could ever get my mind around. Help me to shine brightly in this dark place. Please use me in whatever circumstances I am to draw men to you through the light you have placed in my life. Thank you for being a light in my life and for all the grace you have given me. Amen!

Authority

John 19:9-11

**9 He took Jesus back into the
headquarters again and asked him,
"Where are you from?" But Jesus
gave no answer. 10 "Why don't you
talk to me?" Pilate demanded. "Don't
you realize that I have the power to
release you or crucify you?"**

**11 Then Jesus said, "You would have
no power over me at all unless it
were given to you from above. So,
the one who handed me over to you
has the greater sin."**

One thing men love more than anything is power over other men. All you have to do is look around and you can see this. One time I was working for a man who liked to yell a lot and make threats because he had the power to give employment and take it away. He called me about a problem he was having and began to curse, yell, and scream saying if he had to fire someone, he was going to do it. I don't know why I did it, but I asked him plainly "are you going to fire me? To my surprise he calmed down and said no I am not going to fire you but I don't get my problem fixed, I am going to fire someone. I fixed his problem, and I kept my job, and he calmed down.

While he had earthly power to affect my employment and where my paycheck came from, he did not have the power to affect my Lord from providing for me or my eternity.

Today a lot of us look at the world and worry about those who are in positions of authority over us and how they could affect our lives. Remember the words of the Christ "You would have no power over me at all unless it were given to you from above."

Those who threaten, oppress, abuse, use fear, and the list who goes on have nothing at all. Weather in this life or the next their time will come.

You have a mighty savior in Jesus Christ and He has promised you a glorious eternity. Today walk in that promise. Walk upright and stand tall because you are a follower of Christ, and no man can take that away.

Will you pray with me today? Lord, thank you for ycur grace. Thank you for all you have done for me and all you have planned for me. Let me walk no more in a spirit of fear but rather let me walk in the victory You have won for me. I pray for more of the Holy Spirit to strengthen my walk and my faith today. Amen

Decision Day

Joshua 24:14-15

14 "Now therefore, fear the LORD,
serve Him in sincerity and in truth,
and put away the gods which your
fathers served on the other side of
the River and in Egypt. Serve
the LORD! 15 And if it seems evil to
you to serve the LORD, choose for
yourselves this day whom you will
serve, whether the gods which your
fathers served that *were* on the
other side of the River, or the gods
of the Amorites, in whose land you
dwell. But as for me and my house,
we will serve the LORD."

Bob Dylan famously wrote these lyrics:

You may be an ambassador to England or France
You may like to gamble; you might like to dance
You may be the heavyweight champion of the world
You may be a socialite with a long string of pearls

But you're gonna have to serve
somebody, yes
Indeed you're gonna have to serve
somebody
Well, it may be the devil, or it may be
the Lord
But you're gonna have to serve
somebody

This is the problem in the world today. It is not one political party or another, rich or poor, nor black or white. It is a fact that you have to serve somebody.

Who are you serving today? Right now, as you read this what is your choice for today?

There was a time when most held onto the idea of a creator that we would have to answer too, and this is how they viewed their actions. Now don't get me wrong sin was always present but there was still the ever presence belief of something greater than us.

How do you view your job? How do you view your studies? How do you view your friendships?

Is with the idea that the individual must take a back seat to the greater good of mankind? Wow this does not sound that bad. Think of what we could be if we just served for the betterment of man.

Or is it with the idea that all you do is unto the Creator of all that is and ever will be who sent His one and only Son to take our place of suffering.

Which do you serve? I know the first sounds great. It sounds like the populace message of the world. It sounds like an angel of light!

I know what the second sounds like! It sounds like slavery to a creator who has placed me in a world of suffering. A Creator who has put in place a bunch of rules that no one can live up to. What has this Creator done for us anyways? Look at the state of this world! We need to help society!

Well, I know which I choose! Do you?

Will you follow the populace? Will you use your knowledge, resources, power for the betterment of man? I wonder how this can be if you choose to serve the message of the angel of light instead of the one who created?

Say with me today as you read this, as for me and my house we will serve the Lord! Do everything unto Him who has a plan for you and see how that affects those who think you are serving them.

Let's Pray! Oh Lord, this is so hard to do. I pray for you Holy Spirit to fill me and give me the strength I need to serve you in all I do. Help me to work my best for you! Help me to love my family rightly and the best for you! Help me to honor those who do not deserve it not because of me but because I love you. Thank you that I do not have to serve this world. Thank you for your mercy and provision. Amen

Value

Luke 12:6-7

[6] Are not five sparrows sold for two cents? *Yet* not one of them is forgotten before God. [7] Indeed, the very hairs of your head are all numbered. Do not fear; you are more valuable than many sparrows.

When I was a young boy, I was raised mostly by great Aunt and uncle until the age of nine. That is when my aunt died of cancer. My entire life had witnessed the suffering that came from that horrible disease.

During one tough stretch she was bedridden for several days. It was a night during this time that I was playing in the living room while my uncle watched television, and we heard her yell his name. This wasn't an ordinary yell, and I watched him get up and run to her room while telling me to stay put. I never have been a very good listener, so I snuck around the corner to see her getting out of bed and telling him to go out the alley behind the house and get that man. You see there was a bum rummaging through garbage cans at that moment looking for food and she saw him.

My uncle did as she said and brought him to the house where she proceeded to give him a loaf of bread and make sure he had some food before he went on his way.

It would be easy to say oh how nice or what good would one loaf of bread do but you see I know nothing about that man at all or his circumstances. I don't know if he believed in Jesus or the devil. All I know is at that moment something caused my dying aunt to value that man and provide for him.

I know there are many out there who feel worthless. Feel far less than the two cents it cost for sparrows. I don't know what your circumstances are or what you believe but I do know this in the sight of the Lord you are valuable. Your life could be spent as a beggar on the street corner, or a billionaire hedge fund manager and you are more valuable to the Lord than any amount of silver and gold.

He has designed all of the time for you to know how valuable you are in His eyes and in His kingdom.

So today if you don't believe this ask Him to show you! And today if you are struggling may God put that person, that thing, that moment in your life today to show you how valuable you are.

Pray with me! Lord, please forgive me for believing the lies that I have no value. Lord help me to feel Your great love for me today. Help me to see just how much you value me at this very moment. Thank you for your loving-kindness. Amen!

Not So Hidden

Psalm 119:11

Your word I have hidden in my heart,
That I might not sin against You.

If you're like me you probably have hidden things for safe keeping only to really forgetting about them. Then one day while you are doing something you find it and it brings you some happiness.

I think in a way this is a lot of times our experience with the Word of God. I know people that just seem to be able to quote scripture right of the top of their head and then there are most of us human people that can't always remember what we did yesterday.

So why read the Word then or even try to memorize it?

Just like when you hear a song playing and because of the music you can sing the words but if you were asked to sing them later without the music you couldn't repeat one the Word comes right when you need.

It comes right when the Holy Spirit plays His tune in your mind and heart. You could be in a discussion and then all of the sudden the scripture you needed for that moment to minister comes out of your mouth.

You could be down and discouraged and then all of the sudden a scripture comes to mind and you are encouraged.

This is why we continually read the Word of God because when we do it becomes hidden in our heart. It sits there and works in us until that perfect time for it to come to our mind.

So today do not be discouraged because you have a hard time memorizing scripture or feel like you get nothing out of it. Just continue to read the Word and hide in your heart and maybe today will be the day God calls it out into action.

Let's pray! Lord, help your Word to stick with me today. Help me to speak your word into action today in my heart or in others. I thank you for that the Word is alive and active. Please help me to glorify you today through the hidden word.

Thank you and Amen!

Greatest of All Time

You might have heard the greatest of all time died. He could do things no other man could do. People knew him everywhere he went and oh my to see the crowds. The crowds would gather and sometimes even call and yell his name. He had a profound impact on the world. He changed the lives of many. Some would do anything just to get a glimpse of him in action. He truly was the greatest of all time. I'm sad to see him go. What will we do without him?

His friends have been calling into shows to tell their memories of how they met him or how he impacted their lives. Even his enemies have shown some respect in his death, but he is gone and now what will we do?

Some talk about the great things he did, like the time they were at a party he turned the water into wine. What about that time they were hurting for cash and he said go catch a fish and there it was a gold coin. Then there was the time they were all hungry and multiplied the food.

It just kept coming and we had so much that we had to take it home in barrels. Oh, the stories! When they were all scared because of a big storm, and he just stood up and told it to stop and it did. Wow!

He was greater than any man that ever lived, greater than any fighter who fought in the ring, greater than any orator who ever spoke, he truly was the greatest of all. Others claimed to be him, but no one could match him. He truly was the greatest of all time.

Is it the end for us now that he is gone? As we watch so many forget what he has done. The world looks like a much darker place to come. How will it be without the greatest of all time?

But wait there's more! No, he is not dead after all! He is alive and well today. The darkness has tried to convince us of the death of the greatest of all time, but he is not like any other man who wore that title. No, he is really the G.O.A.T and he will separate his sheep from the goats! He is coming back on a cloud and every knee and tongue shall confess. Then we will know who the Greatest of all Time really is!

You can know the Greatest of all time today. Just call to him and ask him to change you today and see how the greatest replies!

www.ingramcontent.com/pod-product-compliance
Lightning Source LLC
LaVergne TN
LVHW010605160826
845677LV00013B/3244

* 9 7 9 8 8 9 6 1 9 6 0 2 0 *